To Sarah Francis

SEVEN BAGATELLES
for Solo Oboe

1. March

GORDON JACOB

2

2. Elegy

3. Waltz

4. Slow Air

Adagio

5. Limerick

Allegro vivace

4

6. *Chinese Tune*

7. *Galop*

Processed and printed by Halstan & Co. Ltd., Amersham, Bucks., England

Oxford Music for Oboe includes:

J. S. Bach *arr. Lawton*	Jesu, Joy of Man's Desiring
Berkeley	Concerto for oboe Fierce Tears I and II Snake Three Moods
Blackford	Posthumus Leonatus
Butler	Chaconne
Crosse	Ariadne
Duck	Impressions
Eichner *arr. Rothwell*	Concerto for oboe and strings
Gardner	Sonata No. 2 for oboe and piano
Haydn *ed. Rothwell*	Concerto for oboe and orchestra
Hoddinott	Bagatelles
Howells *arr. Shannon*	Six Pieces from Lambert's Clavichord
Jacob	Seven Bagatelles Sonatina Ten Little Studies
Lawton	The Young Oboist, Book 1
Ledger	Warlike Music
Maconchy	Three Bagatelles
Mathias	Oboe Concerto
Pergolesi *arr. Barbirolli*	Concerto on Themes of Pergolesi
Powers	In Shadow In Two Minds
Thackray	Nine Short Pieces from Three Centuries
Vaughan Williams	Concerto for oboe and strings (*oboe and piano reduction*)
Vincent *ed. Pratt*	Sonata in C major Op. 1 No. 6
Walton *arr. Palmer*	An Oboe Album

OXFORD UNIVERSITY PRESS

ISBN 978-0-19-357366-6

9 780193 573666